What people are saying about the poems in **Sensual Spirit**

"What a rapturous book! Chrystine Julian weds wit and wisdom, body and spirit, in these poems. Her warmth and humor and deep insight radiate off every page."
Gayle Brandeis, author of "Fruitflesh, Seeds of Inspiration for Women that Write," "Self Storage" and the Bellwether Prize winner, "The Book of Dead Birds"

"Chrystine Julian is an amazing modern day poet seer."
The Wellness Times

"I describe you to everyone as a modern day Rumi."
Vanessa Reagan, Dance Leader, Dances of Universal Peace

"Wonderful. I like the passion... its lushness."
Eric Ashford - UK contemporary mystic poet

"Wow! That is really beautiful, how sensually delicious, and your metaphors are so lovely and womanly. May I read it publicly?"
Howard Bilow - Poet / Artist

"I read the first two or three poetry writings from your book today.... WOW! Such magic in how you write! It is transforming."
Rachel Forsyth - Laughter Yoga Instructor

"These are awesome. I hope you are collecting them somewhere. They might make a fabulous book one day!"
Janet Marinaccio, Executive Director, Rhythm Gym

Also by Chrystine Julian

Meandering Mindfulness…Poetry from the place where wander and wonder merge

"Chrystine Julian approaches varied topics with courage and finesse, aspects fitting of a great poet. She defends the freedoms we love and champions some extraordinary ones, too. Every page is accessible and clear as she challenges us to develop our own intuitions and insights. My advice is to try it on, read, and then look in the mirror. Chances are, you won't see yourself in quite the same way."
Nancy Krieg, American poet and musician

"Chrystine Julian's poems carve out a space for themselves…one surprising slice at a time. Even the short pieces are mighty in meaning and insight. From the very few lines that embody a world view of trees to the vulnerability of passion and love, Chrystine manages to touch the heart, and intrigue the mind. I highly recommend her lovely book of poetry, *Meandering Mindfulness.*"
Ruth Light
Women's National Book Association

"Chrystine Julian is a unique and personal voice. Her keen eye and ear give lyrical expression to the most ordinary occurrences of life, and her imagination transforms them from the mundane to the magical. In turn she finds in the unusual and extraordinary simplicities that make these events accessible to everyday human understanding."
John Bragin, Core Faculty Member
UCLA Human Complex Systems Program

Long Tongue Love - improvisational percussion
Available on CD and digital download

Sensual Spirit
*poetry and thoughts from the place
where body and soul meet*

by
Chrystine Julian

Edited by Ina Hillebrandt

Sensual Spirit…
poetry for the place where body and soul meet
Chrystine Julian

Edited by Ina Hillebrandt
Cover art by Chrystine Julian
Cover and book design by Chrystine Julian

Second Printing

© 2009, 2007 by Chrystine Julian. All rights reserved. No portion of this book may be reproduced in any form whatsoever without the written permission of Pawpress, except in the case of brief excerpts published in critical reviews or articles. Inquiries concerning all other uses should be directed to Pawpress. https://InasPawprints.com, Brentwood Village • PO Box 492213 • Los Angeles, CA 90049
E-mail: annap@InasPawprints.com

Library of Congress Control Number: 2007922122

ISBN 978-1-880882-11-5

Previously published selections, all © Chrystine Julian, reprinted with permission:
"Reducing Plan**,**" published in *The Messenger,* July 2005
"Fruits of Worldly Love," published in *Poetic Perspectives Anthology,*
    Forward Press – UK, January 2006, and *The Wellness Times,* March 2006
"Dear John Letter," published in *Poppy Fields Anthology*,
    Forward Press – *UK*, September 2006
 "Yosemite to Death Valley", published in *The Wellness Times,* January 2006
"Guarded Heart," published in *The Wellness Times*, January 2006
"Hand of Matches" published in *San Gabriel Valley Poetry Quarterly*

a PAWPRESS book

Printed by Lightning Source, on acid-free paper, from pulp of non-endangered species, non-old growth trees.

Acknowledgments

I offer special thanks to my editor, Ina Hillebrandt. Her insight, guidance, friendship, support and expertise were critical in making this dream a reality. She is a ro in every sense of the word.

I also want to thank everyone that encouraged me by requesting more poems. It is my hope that I will never disappoint you.

Dedication

This book is dedicated to the many people that have broken my heart. Without their help I would have never discovered the mysteries inside that hardened shell.

Thank you!

Foreword

Working with Chrystine Julian on her book of sumptuous poetry has been a dance through rarefied air. Her mind clearly travels on a path all its own, and her observations touch every nerve end, reminding us to think, laugh, revel, and celebrate life.

Ina Hillebrandt, editor of "Sensual Spirit," speaker and author of books including "Pawprints," and "How to Write Your Memoirs... Fun Prompts to Make Writing ... and Reading... Your Life Stories A Pleasure"

Introduction

I was eighteen years old when the phrase "God is love" appeared in my religious experience. That principle remains the one constant in my years of spiritual adventure.

Even a casual reader of mystic poetry and literature will be aware of the connection between sensual passion and the divine. King Solomon and his wives — Rada and Lord Krishna, St. John of the Cross and his beloved, Rumi longing for Shams, The Church as the bride awaiting the return of her groom — are a few examples that link physical ecstasy with enlightenment. It is a perfect metaphor and much more. It is a reality.

Sensuality does not replace or even complement spirituality. Being spiritual is by its nature emotional, tactile, sensitive, intuitive, loving, receiving, giving and all of the other actions and sensations we would roll up under the heading of sensual.

The pieces in this book are meant to be much more than light love poems or erotic stimulation. In reading them, I hope you'll experience my vision of rapture, longing, laughter and social consciousness. These are not intended to be simply pretty words in artful forms. In conception and composition they are sincere revelations and reflections on my experience of life.

It is my hope that this collection touches you in a special way, but I will also be content if you find them simply pleasurable.

Enjoy!

Chrystine Julian

Table of Contents

Sensual
Awakened To Love 1
Hand of Matches 2
Mt. Love 3
Wind of Love 4
The Moon Calls as I Pray 5
Worthy Prey 6
Ears 8
Bedtime Story 9
The Muck of Love 10
Open the Door 12
A Pearl Melts 13
Loving the Lover's Love 14
Blow Through Me 16
Soft 17
Morning Prayers 18
Fruits of Worldly Love 19
Rise 20
Reducing Plan 21
The Dragon 22

Another side of love
Hound 24
Love Left 25
A Bad Poem 26
Love Sucks 27
Dear John Letter 28
Shopping Trip 29
Daughter of Diogones 30
Joe and Jane on Valentine's Day 31
Water Melancholy 32
Food Fetish 33

Pucca of Passion 34
Dam Destroyer 36
Queen of Roses Dethroned 38
Winter Pre-Dawns 39
Loving Meet Longing 40
The Season 42
The Cocoa Was Better 43
Forget We Met 44
Waltzing 45
Short Vacation and Vision Quest 46
Rummaging and Reminiscing 48
No Resistance 50
The Little Shop of Love 51
Love Is Rude 52

Spirit

My Lesson 54
To Know God 55
Conversation 56
The Dive 57
A Drop 58
Uncoiled 59
The Bath 60
Ice Cream 62
Searching for Air 63
Have you Been Told? 64
Tween Space 65
I See You Looking 66
Sky 67
See With Your Heart 68
Fill Your Life 69
Yosemite to Death Valley 70
Play Ball! 72

On Poetry

Secret Agent ... 74
After Sunday School ... 76
Poetry in the Nude ... 78
Metaphor Whore ... 80
The Masterpiece ... 82
Wrestling with Words ... 83
One Liners ... 84

Real Peace Begins Within

Peace Is ... 86
Potholes ... 87
Who Did It ... 88
Drama in Real Life ... 89
Nightmare ... 90
Pissed Off ... 93
F-ing War on Terror ... 94
Questions on War ... 95
Hear That ... 96
Awards and Wars ... 97
Peace Begins Within ... 98

Closing Thought

Kaleidoscope Life ... 101

Sensual

Awakened to Love

The sun comes in without knocking.
Quietly slipping back
my quilted night
and warmly caressing my cheek.
The softest of touches,
nearly a tickle,
a finger traces
to my ear
and down my neck.
It arouses me
with a kiss and a whisper.
A familiar feeling,
I know this glow.
My body arches,
rises and readies
for a day of rapture.
I awaken to love.

Hand of Matches

Hand of matches
via a viaduct
south side entrance
city limits of love
the fingers touch
softer than breath
blown through a
golden gateway
sirens sounding
racing across
an aloneness
bridge to her core
awakened and
alive with fire
desire's inferno
blows the embers
and the flames lick
as tongues of fire
along her sides
around the hills
through the valleys
and burning bush
entering holy ground
take off your shoes
no fire fighting
allowed today

Mt. Love

A soundless whisper on skin
awakens deep strata of soul.
The beloved breathes being.
Tremors foretell the explosion.
With a kiss, I become nothing
real, rationalized or recognized.
Powerful plumes pouring
as molten stone, flowing fire
sliding on slopes of Mt. Love.

Wind of Love

This wind never whispers,
it howls and growls its challenge.
Would you dare dance?

All that is real is rustling with the passing.

It presses close to feel the fleshy firmness
 of your form
and without permission penetrates your
 private places
Would you dare dance?

It is self-important, impatient, impolite
but pointedly passionate.

If you are uneasy or become queasy being
 spun,
if you detest a mess or will not be unkempt
dare not dance this dance.

Crawl into a hole until
the wind of love has passed.

The Moon Calls As I Pray

Passion is persistently pressing
to close off the day.
The moon calls as I pray.
There is no respect for my diligence.
My beloved comes in many forms.
Tonight she is a seductress
demanding surrender.
I require no provocation.
She is swelled to fullness,
prepared even before
I enter her presence.
Her touch awakens the scent of readiness.
It is the aroma
of a night blooming garden.
The air fills with delicious desire.
I sway to breath's rhythm.
Then we dance
to the beat of my heart.
Waves of warmth wash me
as she pulls close and whispers.
The burning boils my blood
and scalds my soul.
She directs me
to mount dreams
and ride the pulsing of her light.
The seduction surrounds and sequesters
my senses.
I cuddle closer,
exploring the secrets
hidden in her form
until she explodes in liquid brilliance.

Then I rest in love.

Worthy Prey

I attempt to run, but my feet
are immovable weights.
A blade of terror severed connections
between body and mind.
I am afflicted by an unpleasant
paralysis without numbness.

In the time it takes a flame to flicker once
the hulking form of hungry love overtakes me.
The chase ends as the beast looms
above my motionless, prostrate body.
Its panting exhalations and musky
scent of sweat choke off my breath.

The monster tears flesh, breaking ribs
and ripping through fat layers of humanity.
I feel pain and blood pulsing in my throat,
legs and secret sacred chambers.
I am surrendered without consent to the fate
of being consumed as a hard earned prize.

In this proximity I can perceive and read
the mind of the monster.
There is no fear, only instinctive hunger.
It has no desire for any part
of my physical existence except
the naturally warmed delicacy of heart.

Suddenly it stops…
backing cautiously away.
The fire of desire was diminished and
extinguished by disappointment.
My life and soul pumping muscle
is not yet large enough for its taste.

The predator form dissolves into a
shapeless shadow evaporated by night.
I am left wishing it would again catch
my scent and start a chase.
I pray for the chance to be pursued
and devoured as a worthy prey.

Chrystine Julian

Ears

I thought ears were for hearing until I met you
An earlobe and diamond stud
Are fondled between thumb and middle finger
As the index digit traces the peach fuzz outline
Lightly a kiss on the spot
Slightly behind and below
The damp touch of the tongue's tip
Blown dry by a whisper of breath
As the other hand reads the epic novel
Written in the Braille of goose bumps
Remembering you makes me
Wish I had larger ears

Bedtime Story

The sun checks out early this time of year.
I pull up my comforter without knowing if or
When the alarm will awaken love again, but
I allow drowsiness to open a book of dreams.

As the room darkens images become bright
In this graphic novel of nocturnal notions from
My favorite author of beautiful bedtime stories.
I am delightfully enlightened by your artistry

There is no hope that you will write me into the plot.
Perhaps I might have fortune to be a bookmark placed
Between the dog-eared pages of fantasy and fulfillment.
Instead of simply another scrap ripped from a rough draft.

The Muck of Love

Prisms of dew create
elaborately flashy jewels.
The swamp of life can be beautiful
in morning sun as the last
of the nightly mist rises
and spreads into nothingness.
I was looking for a path;
something unexplored,
at least by me.

I had been walking
for an unmeasured segment of time,
carelessly taken with sensations
of floral and earthy scents.
The patterns of light and shadow
reminded me of an unnamed abstract
I had seen in an obscure
side street storefront gallery.
Perhaps it had been in Pasadena,
or maybe Bakersfield.

I was unaware that just ahead
pieces of presumed security
had crumbled to grains
and mixed with tears
to form a soggy bog.
Without warning… love
would be sucking hard
and attempting to drag me
deep into its trap.

The first notice was oozing
coolness between my toes.
I stood still enjoying the feeling.
The touch reached up to tickle
my ankles, then knees and thighs.
As it clung and passed my source
of creative and sensual pleasure
and then pulled up to my waist,
I understood that I was stuck.

I could see, but
could not reach the grass
and belly flower lined path.
My past was out of touching range.
Where love grasped I had no sense
except its pressure, presence, and advance.
I knew that soon I'd be consumed.

This whole of passion would
cut off worldly light or atmosphere,
immersing me in an unmarked grave of muck.
Any movement or struggling
would speed the course
of the baptism without resurrection.
So with whatever part
of my body that could be moved

I danced.

Chrystine Julian

Open the Door

There is light shining in your eyes
Within this sacred and holy space
There is warmth radiating in your soul
That I feel in your embrace
Throw open the curtains of your heart
Look at the landscape of love
It invites you to adventure past
Known horizons, below and above

Unlatch the lock,
Open the door and explore

A Pearl Melts

A pearl melts in a glass of wine.
So my heart drops into love
and disappears,
a drink served at the table
of the divine.

There is no distinction
between the beauty
and the fluid.

I am one with all that is.

Loving the Lover's Love

Being the light being
Loving the lover's love
A lifetime in a moment

Consumed by the passion
A moment is a life
Loving the lover's love

Am I too young to know
Can I dare go that far
Will I surrender all
Wrapped within your arms

Electrically you touch me
Unfamiliar places start
To tingle with a longing
As you caress my sacred parts

Being the light being
Loving the lover's love
A lifetime in a moment

Consumed by the passion
A moment is a life
Loving the lover's love

There is nowhere but here
There is no time but now
The passion is our presence
My breath a low growl

I jolt as you enter and melt
Away the dark and cold
Can I be within the being
Can this being be my soul

Being the light being
Loving the lover's love
A lifetime in a moment

Consumed by the passion
A moment is a life
Loving the lover's love

When I am not here
I want to know where I was
When I was here
But when I'm here I do not care

Where is this place this here
I know without my mind
I understand in less than words
Until I'm there not here

Being the light being
Loving the lover's love
A lifetime in a moment

Consumed by the passion
A moment is a life
Loving the lover's love

Blow Through Me

It is the emptiness
The places that I am not
Which make the notes
As your breath flows
Through the hollow
In my soul and
Your fingers dance
Across the holes

Blow through me

Let me be filled
With your song
Let me be nothing more
Than the nothing
With which you make
Beautiful music
Sweet breath of love
Breathe on me

Blow through me

Press your lips
And then empty
All you are into
All that I am not
Let the warm air
From the core
Of your essence
Be my existence

Sweet breath of love
Blow through me

Soft

Soft, ageless and as perfect as an angel's skin,
gentle, careful and cautious as a newborn's nurse,
smooth as melted chocolate, sweet as nearly hard cider,
quiet as the shore of a frozen lake.

I take on the character of the space
and then within the sanctuary of love
kneel reverently at the altar
of your memory.

Morning Prayers

Early morning is when you wake her.
It is not quite night and still not light.
The dense stillness wraps and warms her soul
like thickness of a plush terry robe.

She sips coffee as you rub her neck,
She relaxes in touches of love.
You start holy pleasure in darkness
then welcome the dawn with ecstasy.

Passion is her prayer and offering.

Fruits of Worldly Love

The fruit of worldly love, ripened, sweetened. Then its juice turned to wine. It intoxicated, confused and filled my mind. I stumbled in a stupor, and ignored so much more. My head was filled with hallucinations of passion, of meanings and drunken understandings. There was joy and celebration as I lie puking on the floor. That wine runs dry and winds my mind around its empty flask. I want so much to find a drunkenness that lasts. So I turn to an unworldly fruit, an ecstasy that endures. I drink the wine of divine grapes, always sweet, with no morning after pain. The figments of its fermentation are real and firm. This bottle never empties. I sing drunkard's songs, lost within the verse, wandering the earth.

Should we ever meet, I will offer you a drink.

Rise

Rise and fly - soar high

Love is a soaring soul thing
Leaving the nest of rest
It opens the ring
Of forever together

Rise and fly - soar high

Rising on spirals of rapture
The raptors of passion
Extend their wings of ecstasy
And dance in the wind

Rise and fly - soar high

Ascending above ordinary
Or airy distractions and actions
Beyond clouds of confusion
Looking down on illusions

Rise and fly - soar high

To heaven's home for angels
Watching the unending
Bliss and beautiful happiness
Rising on the thermal of love

Rise and fly - soar high

Reducing Plan

A lesson, I am learning that love is all that matters.
Everything else is just dust in the making.
Love is here, now and forever.
I am on a reducing plan.
Love is all that is.
Love is all.
Love is.
Love.

The Dragon

I was afraid to go out, to love.
There was a dragon named fear
living quite near
my home.
I avoided her for years.

She threatened to destroy
all I owned and all I ever wanted.
Most of the time she slept,
but upon occasion
she would quake and wake,
roaming about igniting bushes and trees.

I could not make her sleep forever.
I could never slay such a huge beast.
So one day as she snored.
I snuck up
and slipped a saddle on her
and cinched it tight.
Then I climbed on
and awakened her for a ride.

When you ride dragons, you fly.

Another Side of Love

Hound

I do not howl at the moon.
I am a hound that's caught
the scent of passing love.
All my senses of instinct
tense and flex leg muscles
pushing to pursue the path.
But I cannot move beyond
the choke chain of social
restrictions and limitation.
I pull at the leash of the past
keeping me staked in the yard
and howl lamentations.

Love Left

Love left,
leaving longing
to linger alone.

The body survives
but spirit dies
in holy demise.

The caesarian
cessation
of life,

supernatural natal,
constructive
destruction,

where it ends
it mends and
begins again.

A Bad Poem

My intent is to write a bad poem.
Well, not really a bad poem.
In fact it may behave quite splendidly.
Actually, I don't want to know it well enough
to make a judgment...
Who would want to hang out
with such a thing?
I'd prefer we just pass in the hall,
say hello, and then move on.

Anyway, the problem is a lover,
actually an ex-lover to be precise.
I need a poem that matches my feelings.
I would not waste good words
or great lines on someone like that.
I need a poem without pattern,
rhythm or rhyme.
I need something that makes you groan
instead of cry.
If someone read it and said,
"Yuck, how awful!"
I'd be content.
Someone could proclaim loudly,
"Bad poem!"
and rub my nose in it.

But as I write,
I see beauty
and feel the universe in union
with the souls of those
separated by physical reality
but joined by silver strands
of love.

Bummer. I suppose I'll need to try
again.

Love Sucks

||
||
||

Don't give me that kind of look
My tears are just love slurping
through a straw. I am drawn up
from the bottom of my glass.
The rude noises are in fact
the sound affects of love.
I am almost emptied.
Sometimes,
to get it all,
love
just
sucks
and
sucks,
and then fills me up again.

Chrystine Julian

Dear John Letter

Read in a shivering cold trench row
Dear John, the name a sharp bayonet
Attacking all for which he'd fought

A veteran's voice comes with advice
Danger may hide in extended loyalty
When an amorous armor fatally fails

Beware what's left as hidden threat
A disguised disfigured memory keeps
Unexploded mines buried on the road

Step away, walking without honoring
An abandoned casualty, those fallen
In a fight for what might have been

Lost love leaves no heroes standing
Refuse to watch them writhe in pain
Lying discarded in trenches of time

Don't hold a bloody corpse too long
There is no sense embraced by death
Or memory cuddled until last breath

Make a shelter within the noisy war
And the battlement of forgetfulness
The voice fades in the battle's din

He is alone, very alone in his hole

Shopping Trip

A trip to the mall
is always a good
choice when she
is feeling low
on self esteem.

She doesn't mind
the traffic or that all
the near spaces
are already taken.
She is not bothered
by the crowds

Doors locked?
  Yes
Windows up?
  Yes
Lights off?
  Yes
Brake set?
  Yes

Check them
again
and then
let go.

The dark corner
of a parking lot
is a good place
to cry
alone.

Chrystine Julian

Daughter of Diogones

Diogones: Greek philosopher and founder of the Cynic School who advocated self-control and the pursuit of virtue through simple living. He is said to have once wandered through the streets of Athens with a lantern in daylight, searching for an honest man. It was said the lantern would light when exposed to truth.

She falls into a generation gap
looking for true and honest love.
Simple virtues and endless searches
are apparently family values.

She is not a virgin of the hearth.
She is a Daughter of Diogones.
He looked for truth and honesty.
Her cynic's search is for love.

She needs someone to light her lamp.
and hates her heritage of doubt.
That was her parent's thing.
In love she longs to be wrong.

Joe and Jane on Valentine's Day

Jane Dough ran into Joseph Blowe at the counter of a coffee stop.

The flames of their affair had gotten so low that the wax was just a shapeless hardened puddle.

For a moment sparks jumped between their eyes only to flatten and become an open can of day old soda, still sweet but no fizz.

They will never name what it was they'd had or lost. It was all impersonal, ordinary with no unique identity.

Joe bought a pink heart-shaped cookie. He took a big bite as he brushed by Jane and pushed through the door without speaking.

He wonders if a Joe Blowe or Jane Dough can ever find love until they discover who they really are.

Water Melancholy

A marine layer hangs low and thick
as a cloudy cap pulled down over her eyes.
It shades the view and mutes the sound of memories.

The melody of her water melancholy
emerged riding on a broken shell that
crashed with the breakers on the rocks.

Dissonant notes reach inward at irregular rhythm.
She wades in tears pooled by the receding passion tide,
singing a song unheard except by the gulls and wind.

It has a familiar feel, but she can't dance to it.

Food Fetish

What's left is not fit for leftovers.
The once crisp allure is oily and limp.
She greets the day like lips licking
salt from a cold french-fry.

She is run down by drive-through love.
Cheap romance is difficult to digest.
The entree she enjoyed is gone
except for the lump in her stomach.

She wants crystal goblet prisms
refracting candle flames preceding
the slow deliberate devouring of
a decadent chocolate dessert.

Still, her unspoken sensual passion
and daydream is breakfast in bed
brought hot and steaming.
She guesses it is all a food fetish.

Pucca of Passion

I walked in still darkness
on a road towards home along
a familiar thoughtless path known well.

Until tonight I was
only vaguely aware
of the vulgar beasts
that frequent this realm.

Hidden by dark camouflage,
she stood blended with the shadows.
I stopped

Then she stepped forward
to stand in my path.
I felt a pulse pumping and burning
my ears and everywhere else.

A cloud slid off the moon
to show her hulking form
as tall and strong.

The headless horse's hoof
scratched the dirt.
I was frozen before the Pucca of Passion
with a dampness in my pants.

All my sense had been
spent on mugs at the inn.
I understood her intent.

She presented not a threat,
but bent to bid me ride the rapture.
Desire unfroze my willingness
As I staggered to her side.

She made it easy for me to mount
and then moved quite quietly and smooth
into the woods, each step building speed.

The forest blurred into a tunnel
of indeterminate pattern.
We emerged at the edge of a cliff
running full gallop where only goats can go.

We raced alone along the rim of the world.
Distant village lights
gave me our bearing of height.

My heart beat as hard as her feet.
Rocks fell loose and rolled
into the blackness off the edge.
I feared our fate was to follow them.

Then we turned into the trail
between the moon silhouetted trees
and bolted back the way we came.

Colorless images blended into
indistinguishably blurred forms.
They passed fast
until we halted at the road.

If a Pucca bids you ride, beware
It's a thrill that takes you high
but leaves you nowhere different.

Once finished it is still a long walk home.

Dam Destroyer

Love,
she held it back and
let it pool into a lake
until it stagnated.
The alkaloid content
built and then killed
anything
that dared grow
in the water.

Most mapped their journey
around the stench.
Then came one,
a person of purpose.
The mischievous missionary
attacked the foundation
of her protection.
Blow after blow of
a jackhammer's drum roll
pounded till it opened
a tiny hole
and started the trickle.

Each drop eroded a piece
of the well poured wall
of artificial stone.
Suddenly the whole
dam thing crumbled.
It released a flood
of destruction
through the valley
that ran on
and was absorbed
in the ocean.

The mud dried.
A new life
emerged.

She smiles at the flowers
and allows all that will stop
to stay awhile and
drink from the water.

She offers a prayer
of thankfulness
to the powerful
and persistent
dam destroyer
that moved on
to another
reservoir.

Queen of Roses Dethroned

Without coronation she was crowned
Queen of the glorious growing bouquet.
For a time she was Potentate of Passion
but even kind kingdoms are taken down
by internal struggle and soul's ugly strife.

Falling then failing in love becomes
an ended reign over wilted roses.
Realization is raised in reality.
Her mind molds to a mob mentality.
Her thoughts take up revolution.
Ragged emotions rally to toss her out
She is dumped tussled and tormented.

This view of beauty is plainly painful.
Dethroned she is thrown on the thorns.
Yet aroused by remembering the rose's
scent and sweet sentiments,
she rises in humility to till the garden ground
while whispering wishes watered by tears and
tended with tender attentions.
The petals of one petite blossom in bloom
will place her on the throne again.

Winter Pre-Dawns

She raced through the night,
beat the sun to the morning
and now waits for it to catch up.
She rustles about
sorting random thoughts
like a drawer of unmatched socks.
Some are dark and tattered
and no two make a pair.
Something about that
reminds her of romance.

Each passing car
is a note in a chord
of cacophony.
Brakes whine because
they are thin
and have pressed beyond
their recommended life span.
That's her love... used,
stopped too often
and needlessly hard.

The shell around her heart
is thin and the insides
have been refrigerated
a bit too long.
She cracks the morning
like a hard-boiled egg
left over from Easter Sunday.
It is there.
She might as well use it.

Winter pre-dawns
are often cold.

Loving Meet Longing

She set up a meeting
for the estranged twins.
It was a momentous
and much anticipated event.

She begins, "Loving
meet Longing.
Longing
this is Loving."

There is
instantaneous
recognition
and reconciliation.

Briefly the siblings
join hands and
just meander about
in joint musing.

Even though
they have been
apart for years,
they need no speech.

They are
two bodies
sharing the karma
of one soul.

In their destinies
most of the days
are meant to be
spent alone.

Their paths again
bifurcate and
make a blunt end
of the reunion.

It is difficult deciding
which one to follow
so she cries
as they part.

She lives vicariously
as the mother
of sisters that
cannot get along.

She can't understand
why twins
tend to think
they are so different.

Although they are grown,
she still
has trouble
telling them apart.

The Season

Silence echoes endlessly down the undecorated hall of her hollow day.

This season is the reason for overindulging on morsels of remorse.

It will, as is tradition, result in emotional heartburn and digestive discomfort.

She chokes on chunks of well-chewed tears that refuse to be swallowed.

Emptiness resonates, returns and repeats as she eats a feast of rejection… alone.

The Cocoa Was Better

Even in midday she enjoys a candle's glow.

When clouds cover up a winter day
she pulls out a comforter of memories
and cuddles herself on the couch.

The cocoa was better when someone else made it.

But... this will get her by for now.
It is not spiked with brandy or as hot,
but it warms her soul somehow

She'll leave the fireplace unlit for awhile.

She knows how to prepare and survive
for all of life's seasons because,
loneliness and love can come and go

like weather.

Forget We Met

Out of kindness and respect
I request we allow
this love to die before
it has a chance to begin.

Please pretend that glance
wasn't a tad too long.
We should be senile about
the shine in your eyes
and the smile too wide.
The joke was funny.
That is the only reason
I laughed

We should start by being
rude and coarse and keep
a distance between us:
be far enough away
that sparks cannot fly.

Ignore the universe's flow
that tangled our driftwood souls
on the riverbank of passion.
We will end as kindling
in a campfire of love.

There is no need to ignite
a fire that too soon
will diminish to an old flame
casting deep shadows of
dark regrets.

You should forget we met.
If I could, I would.

Waltzing

Released…
From a lease
On a love

Hunting…
Homeless heart
Abandoned

Awake…
And awe filled
But lonely

Dancing…
Directed
By delight

Waltzing…
In the square
All alone

Short Vacation and Vision Quest

(a metaphor for love)

It was a short vacation
and vision quest in late October.
A trip though Death Valley
scheduled between Halloween
and the Day of the Dead.

Jiggling on a dirt road,
taking poetic license
with the word road,
graded, sports bra required path
for vehicular use is more precise.

It transitions by way of a mountain pass
to be a steep loose sand and rock
descent through pupil dilating,
eons as artist, sculpted splendor shape
and odd but natural landscape.

No time for thought, but I
am acutely aware of surroundings
and the energy of the experience:
hairpin turn at a cliff's edge,
heavy breathing from fear
and rarely viewed hidden beauty

I am traveling along a creek bed
with a few boulders removed.
Looking at flowers clinging in cracks,
sky scraping sides of a slashing wound
in the earth that requires no healing.

I slowly continue to wind and descend
until I slide out of the canyon where
the desert vista again pours itself to fill the horizon.
Now I can think, but I cannot believe that
I saw what just passed through my life.

I move back into the salt flat desert
with appreciation, vivid memories
and my capacity for wonder deepened.
I think, how unusual it is that
exploring remote regions seems to be
a lot like love.

I drive home alone.

Rummaging and Reminiscing

Rummaging and reminiscing
through shoe box memories
I recall love flaring
like a photographer's flash:
brightness captured a smile
then left me in shadows.
Faded pictures remain
bound by red and silver ribbons
with assorted letters and cards
of deep but fleeting passion.
I unfold a note crisp from age,
read and remember the distant
dismembered past.

Love Colors Me
Your love colors me like
the effects of the sun setting
and setting the clouds on fire
or turning the plum purple to blue
as it yawns and stretches into day

These are easy to toss
but impossible to release.
On more than one occasion
I have pulled them from the trash.
Hope lives between the lines.
As I have been loved before,
perhaps I may repeat it.
Every grand miracle
deserves a reprise.

I fondle a testament,
a forgotten covenant,
inscribed on a
table napkin tablet

One Love
Pure Love
Real Love
Your love
In love
True love
Hot love
New love

Chrystine Julian

No Resistance

I am a lover with no lover to love
Such things confound and disappoint my mind and tongue

Words and all vacated the place leaving a persistent vacuum
Sometimes life just sucks

Let the beauty we love be what we do?
Let the beauty we are be what we love

A smile sneaks onto my face
I resolve to not resist

The Little Shop of Love

A bell tinkles as she enters
a boutique of love.
Sandalwood and jasmine scents
enchant and enhance the mystery
of this merchant's wares.

She is greeted by a pleasant smile
from behind a counter,
but without an offer of assistance.
Racks hung with colors
are full and displayed
in simple coordinated arrays.
She briefly looks but
then leaves in disappointment.
There appeared to be little there
that fit her size
or fashion requirements.

It just shows that there is much
she cannot know from
a quick shopping trip.
There is a storehouse full of passion
but limited room to show it.
The warehouse has endless rows,
but she will not see it
until she befriends the owner.

Chrystine Julian

Love Is Rude

Some relatives you just have to excuse.
Love is rude.
It knows no manners.
Even with an appointment, it is late or comes too soon.
I have no time to prepare.
It is not fair.
It enters as if it owns this home, just barges in.
It goes to my private room.
It lounges on my bed and demands to be fed.
I need to sleep
but it fills me with wine, then dances all night.
It calls my friends and invites them to party.
They sing loud songs
and leave a mess.
I cannot rest and
I may never get this nest
in order.
I leave for work.
It tags along,
uninvited.
It says things at inappropriate times.
And it will not put away that silly grin.
It embarrasses me.
I blush. I am sorry if it bothers you.
I apologize for this love.
It is just uncivilized.

Spirit

My Lesson

My lesson for today:
(and every day)
Love is eternal,
ever present,
not limited by body
or form;
the universe is one love.

As we live and
are present in it,
we are in love,
are loved,
are made
and supported by love.

No person changes,
adds or detracts from that love.
They simply open our eyes
to see it
and open our hearts
to feel it.

If we live with an open heart,
we live in love.
Each day is a love embrace,
a love emergence
and love immersion.

Today I will live in love.

To Know God

If you would know God,
fall deeply, madly
and passionately in love.

In that moment
you will understand more
than you could learn
from a lifetime of meditation
or religious study.

Conversations

There is a language of love
that has no words and no touch
except for a gaze that carries
light to the depth of the well
and reflects on the smooth surface
of sweet water.

What is seen
is that which is looking.
I pray that we may
communicate
in that way
today.

Our souls desire deep
conversations.

The Dive

In some rarely remembered dream
I let my soul fly.
I stood on a cliff's edge.
The gauze dress pressed
to my skin by the wind.
I leaned forward ready
to fall to whatever becomes
of the fallen.

I didn't push.
There was no jump or jerk,
I just let the smooth motion
leave the ground behind.
I released expectations,
knowing full well
that this was an end.

Night dies in the morning's light.
I became the sunrise
as I allowed my body
and all that I am to rise in the sky.
I am leaning into love today.

Chrystine Julian

A Drop

I am a drop
in the ocean of love.
The river of life is flowing to me.

I am lifted to float,
am a billowy cloud.
I am the rain of liquid love.

The stream gives drink
to life on the ground.
The streams join

to form the river of life
flowing to the sea.
And I become a drop

in the ocean of love.

Uncoiled

You are music.
The song reaches deep.
It calls me.
Uncoiled I sway.
I dance.
You raise the color of life.
As a snake that has been
too long in its basket.

Chrystine Julian

The Bath

Today I light a candle
and draw a bath.
Stripped to the flesh,
I throw my old clothes on a pyre.

My skin aches for the warming
whirlpool of love.
I slide into the tub, so warm, no, so hot,
the lobster in a pot.

At first I recoil
but sit tight knowing I will adjust.
Light swirls around with force
and loosens the crust.
A hand rubs me with a stiff brush.

Washing away the ages
of dirt, mud and dust.
The pulsing massaging my aches,
I begin to relax,
but then shock
when the cleansing does not stop.

My skin itself begins to flake.
It looks so old floating away.
Next my muscles melt and the
marrow and the bone.
I am no more the body that I've known.

The light filters and clears
and becomes a pool of white.
I look to find myself,
hoping I have not drowned.
My skeleton is brilliance,

and my flesh and muscle
layer light upon light.
I am bathing in the tub of love
as it cleans and renews.

I will rest in this bath,
until the process is through.

Ice Cream

The heart's contemplation
confounds the mind.
I fell into a bucket
of newfound love
and am spun around
and around until I am
solid in this space.

Ancient passion
made fresh each day.
The universe
has impeccable taste.
Today it wants ice cream.
The touch melts
my frozen sweetness.

I am licked to the bottom of my cone.

Searching for Air

I am spending my life
searching for air.
My body craves it.
I have been told
that I can't live without it.

How can I look for
what I cannot see?
And that which I can see
I do not want.

It is such an odd quest
upon which to be put.
Still I set all else aside
until I find it.

I am tired from this restless
endless searching.
I am lucky I have not been assigned
to look for God.
How hard would that be?

I think I'll sit here and catch my breath.

Have You Been Told

Have you been told?
Do you know?
You are the one.
You bring light into shadowy corners.
You reach where another may never go.

Did you know you are the anointed one?
Each of us is the one to someone.
You may be the only smile they see today
or the only kind word this week.

Their smile is the mirror where your love primps.
Make it look good today.
To that someone,
you are the chosen one.
Many of the names are not exchanged.
They are faces fading in the night.
Still you are their miracle, just because you are here.

Today, you are the enlightened one to me.

Tween Space

She stands in the doorway
as if an earthquake
is destined to shake her paradigm
and make her uncertainty certain.

By choice every piece is complete and separate.
Her days are night and evenings are dawns.
Her twilight never passes
beyond this tween space.

She lives in the shaman's shadow world,
in between the past and future.
It is a slot that is neither real nor unreal.

She is in the threshold that connects
life to death, past to present and
reason to insanity.
Each is equally her domain.

She is all and none at once.
The loneliness of the universe
occupies the entire space of fulfillment.

With only one step she'd be in a room,
not her own or her home.
So she retreats to this refuge.

To be something or nothing
as an act of will is still
her most prized skill
and preferred position.

Chrystine Julian

I See You Looking

The night has eyes and so does the sky
Watching and watching over me

Their staring is never ending.
I am looking back.

In kind behind I find God's mind.
Watching and watching over me

Yes, I feel the lingering look.
The all of life is a small hall.

Your eyes are sky filled by sunlight.
Watching and watching over me

No intrusion is intended,
just watching you watch.

It appears tonight God's eyes are on loan to you.
Watching and watching over me

Sky

I have known her
As Aditi, Frigg,
Ianna, Nut, Nyx
And many other AKAs

I awake to a sky
Dressed in
Reversible bright
Lazuli robe
When she turns it
Inside out it is
an ebon fabric
Revealed to have
Uneven polka-dotted
Holes which
Let light poke
Down at me

I admire her attire
But my aspiration is
To see her naked
And touch the pulse
Of her heart
As I search for
Secret spots of sensation
Tangling bodies together
In satin sheets
On an embroidered
Pillow layered
Bed of eternity

Chrystine Julian

See With Your Heart

See with your heart
and you will have beauty before you.

Let your soul speak of beauty
and you will never be short of words.

Pray with those words
and you will always have joy.

Be filled with joy
and your heart envisions love.

Break the circle of love
and extend it to an ascending spiral.

Fill Your Life

Fill your life with beauty.

Permit it to crowd you
as it permeates with awe.
Let it be so close
you can barely breathe.

Marvel at intricate detail.
Gasp at the way it feels.
Evoke joy, tears or laughter,
each in a unique way.

How you see it
is how the universe sees you.
Perhaps you will understand
it is the mirror of your soul.

You are beauty in my world.

Yosemite to Death Valley

It was good to have a couple
of days all to myself
and to fill them with beauty.

Fire inspired colors hung on trees,
large rocks, lava fields, deep shadows,
deeper canyons, contented cattle grazing,
water running, falling, singing
and pooled into lakes.

Physically and metaphorically,
it was high above the ordinary world
and below it as well.

It would be cruel
to litter it with my troubles,
so I left them
in a canister somewhere
along the way.

In those places I am content
to be a recipient of simple gifts.

It was an unfair poetry competition
for which I was ill prepared.
The mountain, river or desert
do not appreciate my poetry.
Although they do hope I like theirs.
It is shared whether or not I care.

I became a sacred cow
in a divine ranch roundup.
I was culled from the herd,
roped and tied by vision
and then branded by love
that pierces through my eyes.
Images burned their mark
on my soul and mind.
I am released back to my field
knowing to whom I belong.

At once I am small
on the landscape of grandeur
and huge as I merge
to be one with it all.

Perhaps that is how
we are with God.

Play Ball!

They tell me that in the beginning
God created a baseball game.
He bulldozed a pasture
and made a diamond,
set up the fence, baselines and backstop.
From the dust he picked the teams
and set the rules of play.
Then he went up to the stands
and took a seat from which to keep score

It seems to me to be a silly game,
so I sit in right field
watching the action.
When it is my turn at bat,
don't expect me to swing.
I won't run or take a walk,
so call me out on strikes
I am too busy reading
the testaments that are scribbled
on the grass and inscribed
on the tablets of dandelions.

On Poetry

Secret Agent

There is not much time
so I must say this quickly.
I have been conscripted
for an intelligence mission.
I am going alone under covers
in the dark city of dreams.

My briefing says:
"We fear forces are
seeking to seize control.
Early reports indicate
they are stockpiling
caches of passion.
If left unchecked
the pile will grow,
and explode
in an episode
of world peace.
The fallout could
disrupt all life
as we know it.
The mundane might
never be the same
again."

Thus, my
must-do mission:
I am to infiltrate
the secret circle,
return information.
and if I can,
understand
the pending plans
and motivations.

I'll be a clandestine
data collector
and disguised
goal miner.

Please be ready to
receive and review
current reports.
I'll be sending them
cloaked within
poems and coded
in cryptic verses.

Chrystine Julian

After Sunday School

After Sunday school she had time
to reflect and journal thoughts.

Bodies are temples of God,
with the exception of the basement.
Don't go down there.

It is dirty, dark and stinky
or so they tell her to think.

She nibbles lunch as she writes.
Life is food, giving nourishment to grow,
undigested portions must be disposed.

Leaning back to reflect, she hopes
one day to write a poem about the crap.

She wants to spell the words without worry,
where there's no adolescent giggling at bodily gurgling
or disapproval of righteous religious dignitaries.

She desires to speak in metaphors
of the most common denominators,

Emotions and compassion
get bound up, backed up, built up
until they bulge and explode.
She hates cleaning up those messes.
She writes again, deal with your shit.

Then thinking,
when she has had an emotional movement,
washed and come clean, she might be
open to spend time exploring
what other precious treasures
that basement might be storing.

She closes the journal
pulling her knees up to her chest.
She dares not write or think the rest.

Poetry in the Nude

Would it bother you
if I presented my mind
as a nude?
Do I need
some sort of excuse?
Is it rude?
Will you accuse me
of mental perversion?

What if there is no style
to make it attractive
and no fashion interaction?
Imagine a train of thought
with nothing sucked in.
What then
will it be?

If it greeted you at the door
with no disguise…
would you be surprised?
Would you be offended
or see it
as an invitation
to sensation?
Would you give an order
to cover up the expanse
of all that nature has given?

We dress our contemplation
to impress
with success
in accumulation
and beg for adulation.
Then we bend and twist
to girdle our thoughts
within the latest trend.

I have been
there
and must say
never again
to that terrible sin
of constriction.

I'll not make an apology
if it agitates
religious mythology
or standard decency.
That is simply
not my concern.
In turn,
I expect no respect,
just the space
where I can wear
all that God has given me.

(Lala, we love you.)

Chrystine Julian

Metaphor Whore

A soul mate left her
with no skills but these.
She is desperate
to discover
a means to support
and care for
her own needs

This passion
is a perfected talent.
She surrenders
to selling
her body of work
if that's
what it takes
to survive.

Without reservation
or expectation
but weighted with
anticipation
she descends to
a bohemian basement
brothel of sensual verse.
Perhaps this is a place
she could work.

Pushing up cleavage
to cover her heart
she marches
to the mistress
and with delicate detail
makes a proposition
pronouncing proficiency

at compositional
copulation.

Fulfilling
fancy fantasies
as a whore bejeweled
in words,

she thrives.

The Masterpiece

To master a piece of poetry
or any sort of art
is to have tamed a wild beast.
Then it must be named
and displayed
as your David,
Sunflowers self-poured-trait
or Mona Lisa.

It must be more
than ordained airy words.
It must hang in admiration,
lynched for public
gratification and adulation.
You amputate more than an ear.
Your heart is sacrificed to needs
of appreciation and recognition.

Or perhaps they'll treat your
sacred contribution as
a creative abomination.
The fickle critics fondle
your masterpiece with
jaded contemplation
to justify rejection.

Art lives wild beyond the cage.
It roams and feeds in need of survival.
The master cherishes independence.
The pieces mark her territory.
Surrounded, she calls this home.

Wrestling With Words

Her mind is frayed, confused
frazzled, dizzy and has blown a fuse.
She needs a new word for beautiful,
but all she can write is… you.

One Liners

Love is a rising sun, large on the horizon, but hotter in mid-course.

Love is the broth that heals a coughing heart.

The heart is a blossomed bud releasing a call for the hairy legs of bees to stir and mingle its pollen.

Passion is a ninety proof distilled spirit of love.

Joy is the popping of life's corn.

*Real Peace
Begins Within*

Peace Is

Peace is perennial
Peace is not a seasonal whim. It is meant to endure.
Peace is parental
Peace is the obligation to nurture as well as protect.
Peace is public
Peace is not to be secretive or hidden.
Peace is private
Peace begins within.
Peace is pertinent
Peace is always relevant.
Peace is patient
Peace is not a shallow hurried thing.
Peace is passionate
Peace must be an emotional motivator.
Peace is persistent
Peace pushes and pushes again until its flowers meet the light of day.
Peace is primal
Peace is the essence of our survival skills. We live best when we live in peace.
Peace is the priority
Peace first, peace always.
Peace is pungent
Peace demands our attention.
Peace is never punitive
Peace can never be used to punish.
Peace can be painful
Peace is never given easily or achieved without sacrifice.
Peace is patriotic
Peace is the highest service and the greatest security for our country.

Potholes

I have learned to appreciate the diversity of life and those that live it. Once upon a time in a place far, far away I thought I knew something. I was certain that I had answers for any question. Often time I didn't need the question to have an answer. So long as I was right, the world was good.

Since then I've learned that there are too many questions and too many answers for one mind to own. The individual nature of our queries and answers contribute to the hue that colors our world. We dwell on a world that is shifting and translucent.

It is like oil film on a pothole of water. As a child I loved to go outside after our frequent summer rains. The smell and feeling were delightful. Our street had spots that accumulated water. The film from the road would float across the surface. The light would break across it like a liquid prism in shifting patterns of color.

The oil and the water would never truly mix. Still the oil or water alone had no brilliant color. It was only as they came together that the beauty happened.

Chrystine Julian

Who Did It

Milk of human kindness
with lactose intolerance:
lack of social tolerance
stinks.

It may be hard
to accept and digest,
but don't blame them
for your internal rumbling.
There are those that dine
and delight on difference.

If you can't stomach it
it is not their problem
until you release
loud rudeness in response
to their natural nature.

Please don't do it here.
People will look at you
with twisted faces
and turn away their noses
because it smells atrocious
and they all know
who did it.

Drama in Real life

Curtain opens on a scene of
desolation busted bubbles
security folded in knots
stomach and neck tensions twisting
irreverence of innocents
searching through rubble for what was.

They are wandering in places
once foreign and still wondering
at a distance if they can ever
salvage a life of normalcy.
Wearing the mask of tragedy
shaping frozen frown dialogue.

Improvisational and free
movement sets scenes of suffering.
By bomb or by wind the show blows
into town and has been on the
road in the longest tour for years,
playing command performances.

Indonesia, Somalia,
South Asia, Congo, Palestine,
Baghdad, Kabul, Oklahoma,
London, Beirut, New York City,
New Orleans and then summer stock
in some obscure smaller venues.

Each staging features local casts
of fledgling amateur actors.
This is their chance for attention
before the world audience.
All wish they had skipped auditions.

Chrystine Julian

Nightmare

In a restless nocturnal struggle
she is tossing and rolling
until exhaustion matures
enough strength
to wrestle her down
and pin her beneath its weight.

Dreams can be cruel
to a sleeper's
defenseless mind.
Here visions
have free reign
to play their
bully games.

The powers that be lie
waiting to spring
from the shadows
in attempts
to make her believe
in a war that feeds
a need for power
and gasoline.
She is chased, trapped
and then forcefully
penetrated by their ideas.

Dreams know no disgrace.
While managing
to keep a straight face,
a kindly looking,
but unkind man
offers her candy
and then tells her
it makes the world
a safe place
.

Then comes a teary chorus
of a thousand deceased
that vehemently disagree.
They sing haunting questions.
Is it a better society
because you have
no respect for lives?
Is it preferred
only because you survived?

Her frightful figment fades
and shifts its story line
to become an old fable.

A patriarch parades in pride
wearing the fashionable facade
his tailors of trouble have sewn.
Can they not see?
Do they not know?
The empire has no clothes.

She awakes wiping
crusty sand from her eyes
and shaking off the spell
of the fitful night.

She is grateful
to live in a world
where none of that
could be true.
She brews a cup of joe
and turns on the morning news.

The night's images fade
but their intensity lingers.
It seems…
that not all nightmares
are confined to dreams.

Pissed Off

Leg raised, a dog marks its territory.
This beast pisses bombs.

Can we release the pride and the need to get even?
No one ever wins at war. They only shift the power
and oppression towards different directions.
Violence is always vile and offensive regardless of intention.

Exposed by hindsight and revelation, without exception,
brutality hurts and heightens hate to hideous levels.
Why must we continue to foul our own nest?
When will we be willing to clean up this stinking mess?

F-ing War on Terror

To make a war on terror,
to me, is filling
fire extinguishers with gasoline.
I interchange two letters.
Small changes make a big difference.
I replace the n in on with f
and find my greatest fear.

We've lost the wars on poverty,
drugs and many others.
Still they are declared to be chariots
of salvation and protection.

They do not mend
but rather extend
and then append to sorrow.
A piece of peace
is body-bagged
in each battle.

Our feelings grow cold
until they freeze-dry our freedom.
Then that cracks and crumbles
with the slightest touch.
There is no reconstituted brew
for us to enjoy and left unchecked
no constitution left to protect us.

I'd prefer declaring a peace on war.
Peace and love are pillows
that suffocate hate.

There is no I in war,
and no winning either.

Questions on War

Communication, conversation, one world.
So many voices to be heard.

We've had two world wars.
When do we get our first World Peace?
We've been gorged on war we need a diet of peace.
Obese on war, diet of peace.

Communication, conversation, one world.
So many voices to be heard.

We have so many bombs. Can I trade some for food?
I don't understand. Can you please help me see?
God, did you really tell them they could kill me?

Communication, conversation, One World.
So many voices to be heard.

Hear That?

Do we watch the news
with the sound turned down?
A tree falls and there is no noise.
Is it because none is there to hear
or because
we chose to watch
it on the screen
and not listen to the
screams
of war?

Many have fallen
in clear-cut cities.
Did we hear that?
Does the heart need a hearing aid?

A child, mother, father,
sister or brother dies
and there is no sound of cries
unless the relatives are ours
and they all are
relative.
The rockets' red glare
bombs bursting to bare
our souls.

Each ghost must be a banshee.
When we can no longer stand
the shattering shriek
perhaps then we will stand
and roar "NO MORE!"

Awards and Wars

We watch people glitter, very pretty
and cheer for champions of celebrity

If all the children, mothers,
grandmothers, fathers
and grandfathers
for one day could be gorgeous
perhaps we would stop the slaughter.

I wish that all could see
how beautiful they are to me

Peace Begins Within

For peace
I've looked around and then around again.

War goes on but where does peace begin?
On the fields of fighting
In the temples and towers
The answer of the ancient wisdom
whispers on the wind,
Real peace begins within,
Within.

For war
They march in step, in honor to their drums
From one encounter to another, never to be done.

Even when the drums of war
Are beating all around there is a place
where peace can be found.

Real peace begins within,
Within.

Closing Thought

Kaleidoscope Life

A kaleidoscope life:
uneven and even unfair

broken pieces shifting
mixed in reflection,

every turn a new beauty
when pointed to the light.

Percussion as Poetry

A CD with the passion of Chrystine's poetry expressed by rhythmic voices of instruments from around the world

Available at iTunes, Amazon.com and other digital music download sites

Other books you might find of interest, from Pawpress

Meandering Mindfulness… Poetry from the place where wander and wonder merge, by Chrystine Julian. "Chrystine Julian approaches varied topics with courage and finesse, aspects fitting of a great poet. She defends the freedoms we love and champions some extraordinary ones, too…My advice is to try it on, read, and then look in the mirror. Chances are, you won't see yourself in quite the same way." *Nancy Krieg — American poet and musician*

Pawprints by Ina Hillebrandt, Amazon.com top seller featured on ABC Nightly News, PBS, etc. From "Moonlit Fox" to "Nose Fur," more than 100 short, short "tails" of close encounters of the furry kind. Uplifts, inspires readers to write, and promotes kindness to animals. Purr-fect gift for animal lovers and pets of all ages. "The stories make you feel you are right there…I love them!" Teresa Proscewitz, Chief Forester, City of LA Dept. of Recreation and Parks. ISBN 1-880882-01-9.

The Student Prints, Educators' Guide to Pawprints Literacy Plus™ —The Innovative Standards-Based Literacy and Environmental Program. © 2001 Ina S. Hillebrandt. Companion curriculum guide to *Pawprints,* developed following Pawprints Literacy Plus training module for Jane Goodall Institute. For teachers and parents, grades 1-8, and ESL. "*Pawprints* is a new form of great literature...the book and these exercises have the power to change the way kids…and…adults think." Maxwell Yerger, Reading Specialist/Teacher/Trainer, New York. ISBN 1-880882–03-5.

How to Write Your Memoirs — Fun Prompts to Make Writing … and Reading …Your Life Stories a Pleasure! by Ina Hillebrandt. Easy steps and prompts to make organizing those scraps of paper — physical and mental — fun and rewarding, for the writer, family and friends, and possibly, the public! ISBN 1-880882-04-3. "The questions make it easy!" *Gertrude Brucker, Member, Felicia Mahood Senior Center, Los Angeles*

Stories From The Heart, Volumes 1-3 … Selected stories to delight and inspire readers to create their own memoirs and fiction.
      Vol. 3 Includes writing tools and carefully selected memoirs -- and fiction! -- to entertain, and help readers craft their own enchanting life histories. *"Multi-hued, textured tales – from such stuff was woven the American Dream." Marvin J. Wolf, Author of Fallen Angels and many other nonfiction books.*

Vol. 2, From great grape fiascos to wars...Wit and wisdom by the Pawprints Writing Club (now Footprints) became an **Amazon.com top seller.** Poignant, funny, tender, frightening, insightful memories of the holocaust, flying a plane, bees, first love, South Africa, India in the time of the Raj, cookies and much more. *"The section I most enjoyed was a few punning stories about cats by the late Earl Boretz...most amusing. His characters include Count Fe-Line the cat burglar in Pussy footin' around; Sinister, the three-legged pirate cat and Sorrowful, the witch...Overall, an entertaining collection."* Cecilia Blight, Nelm News, newsletter of The **National English Literary Museum**, Grahamstown, S. Africa.

Vol. 1 features the first delightful tails by Earl Boretz, plus the special whimsy of Arabella Bel-Mitchell, a British lady with an outrageous sense of humor and fantasy, along with lyrical and heartfelt memoirs by authors from various walks of life.

All three ***Stories*** books compiled and edited by Ina Hillebrandt. Vol. 1 ISBN. 1-880882-07-8. Vol. 2 ISBN 1-880882-08-6 Vol. 3 ISBN 1-80882-04-3.

Go East, Young Man, Go East! Memoirs of an eyewitness to the oil boom and culture clashes of the Middle East. By Charles Alan Tichenor, Edited by Ina Hillebrandt. A book of memoirs penned by a witty and informed hand, with tales of political intrigue, spies, cultural exchanges and the effects of black gold on royalty and desert-dwelling Bedouins. ISBN 1-880882-09-4.

Edited by Ina Hillebrandt, Published by Angel Fire Publications

***The Angel Chronicles,** by J.K. Johnson.* A compelling murder mystery/romance with feet in this world and another plane. Written originally from behind prison bars, this page turner by a multi talented woman inspires readers to say, "It's a life changer! And a great read." ISBN 978-0-9819193-0-0.

To order any of our books, please visit Amazon.com
or your local bookstore.
Also available
**Memoir and Fiction Writing workshops and
coaching by Ina**
For more information, and for bulk orders, please visit
our website http://www.InasPawprints.com

Chrystine Julian is a poet, mystic, musician, drummer, drum circle facilitator, and workshop leader.

Her programs include:

Team – Tribe
Team Building with rhythm

Talking Your Power
Put your power where your mouth is.

Sacred Space Community Dances
Sacred ceremony in dance

Sex and the Shaman
Recapturing our bodies and power

She can also be found performing and reading her poetry at various venues around Southern California.

Information is available at

ChrystineDrums.com

e-mail: LadyLovesDrums@aol.com

www.ingramcontent.com/pod-product-compliance
Lightning Source LLC
LaVergne TN
LVHW052101090426
835512LV00036B/3034